TRADITIONAL ENGLISH GARDENS

TRADITIONAL ENGLISH GARDENS

Text by
Arabella Lennox-Boyd
•
Photographs by
Clay Perry
•
Foreword by
Graham Stuart Thomas OBE VMH DHM VMM

A Seven Dials Paperback

First published in the United Kingdom in 1987 by
George Weidenfeld & Nicolson in association with
The National Trust for Places of Historic Interest or Natural Beauty
36 Queen Anne's Gate, London SW1H 9AS

This paperback edition first published in 2003 by
Seven Dials, Weidenfeld & Nicolson
Wellington House, 125 Strand
London, WC2R 0BB

This edition printed 2003 for Eagle Editions Ltd,
11 Heathfield, Royston, Herts SG8 5BW, UK

A CIP catalogue record for this book is available
from the British Library.

ISBN 1-84188-219-4

Filmset by Deltatype, Ellesmere Port Cheshire
Colour separations by Newsele Litho Ltd
Printed and bound in Italy

Half-title page: Mottisfont Abbey, Hampshire
Frontispiece: Blickling Hall, Norfolk
Page 6: Hidcote Manor, Gloucestershire
Page 8: Moseley Old Hall, Staffordshire

· Author's Acknowledgements ·

I would like to thank John Sales, Chief Gardens Adviser, and the tenants, gardeners and staff of the National Trust for their help in checking the manuscript and in providing information. I am indebted to Graham Stuart Thomas for writing a foreword. His own *Gardens of the National Trust* was a helpful guide and his learned books on roses have been an inspiration ever since I started designing gardens. Finally, I am deeply grateful to my husband, Mark, for his constant support, and to my editor, Felicity Luard.

· Photographer's Acknowledgements ·

I would like to thank my wife Maggie for her help and encouragement while preparing the photographs for this book and also the administrators, gardeners, tenants, and staff of the National Trust Information Service who helped to make this book possible. With special thanks to: Stephen Adams, Mr and Mrs James Benthall, Ted Bullock, Mr Harris, Mrs Margaret Hemmings, Jock Henderson, Mr J. Honour, Steve Ingram, Mr M. Jessup, Professor and Mrs J. Malins, Mr and Mrs Stanley Middlemiss, Paul Nicholls, Cavan O'Brien, George Peeling, John Sales, Lt Colonel T. Slessor, John Strickland, Ken Vaughan, Robert Walber, David Weller, Mr and Mrs M. Wrench, Mr and Mrs J. D. Wrisdale.

Contents

List of Gardens

FOREWORD

by Graham Stuart Thomas, OBE, VMH, DHM, VMM
Gardens Consultant to the National Trust

Ham House, Surrey

It gives me the greatest pleasure to look through this book and to be reminded of the numerous gardens where I have spent so many happy days helping and advising the National Trust. Apart from those gardens which are entirely formal in design, Clay Perry's photographs record a main or axial view on which hang all the other visual delights. We have very often a hint of these many extras in Arabella Lennox-Boyd's comments and word-pictures of the gardens. The more we look at the photographs and read the detailed captions the more we realize what infinite variety lies in this remarkable assembly of gardens.

I use the word assembly very guardedly. It is of course true to say that the gardens of the National Trust represent the greatest collection of gardens ever held by one body. But it is not just a collection. It is a remarkable assembly of gardens great and small in which you may trace all the styles and characteristics of garden design over the last three to four hundred years – from Elizabeth I to Elizabeth II – and which contains an unparalleled range of plants.

Most gardens look at their best at midsummer, but there is also a wealth of flowers throughout the season from early bulbs and shrubs until the leaves fall in the splendour of their autumn tints. Apart from the obvious trees and shrubs, planted long ago, which help to make the framework, there are the smaller plants treasured perhaps by families for countless decades which today may have become rare and much sought after. Plants of all kinds are what gardens are principally made for: without plants there would be no gardens. In England the climate allows us to grow a vast range of species from all parts of the Temperate world, both north and south. Even so, like a picture, plants need a framework of design; they need the setting of paths and lawns, hedges, walls and steps to give the reason and the stability for their arrangement. Nowhere, I think, will this be more apparent than in the views here depicted, whose firm lines invite the flowing beauty of plants to embellish them.

On going from garden to garden, from county to county, it will become apparent how often the English yew is chosen for hedges. Undoubtedly it provides the most retiring dark green surface when well clipped, and the best contrast for other foliage and also for flowers. The use of hedges is indeed commonplace for garden boundaries and divisions. Over the centuries, however, craftsmen used their local stone, brick or paving for small terraces and larger landscape design. So materials vary from one garden to another; an appreciation of this can add immeasurably to our enjoyment. The granites and sandstones, shales and limestones all have their unique part to play in garden making, their effect in many ways equalling the importance of the properties of the soils which dictate so closely the choice of plants. The soil and local conditions are not, however, the only things which indicate what plants are to be put into a garden. Each garden has a style of its own and for these styles certain plants would be particularly appropriate, others out of place.

The gardens selected to enhance this book are, mostly, in good order, though sometimes disasters may happen – trees fall, illness may affect the staff and vital machinery may break down. It has always been so, but in spite of all such disadvantages I have watched our gardens improve in interest and upkeep for more than thirty years. Some were in poor condition when accepted by the Trust but were valued highly on their own account or because they acted as a setting to a house of historic importance. It has been my privilege over the years to help and guide the Trust in the restoration of its gardens, though sometimes in highly adverse circumstances. For instance, this book gives a preview of one garden, Biddulph Grange, which has been offered to the Trust but which at the time of writing is in a woebegone state, owing not so much to neglect but to depredations by trespassers and vandals. It may be some time before it can be safeguarded, restored and opened to visitors. I recall how sad I was to come to the garden at Benthall Hall, famous in the past, before the donor had been able to help to restore it; to Cliveden where the planting of rhododendrons had taken precedence over the upkeep of the immensely historic layout; and to Felbrigg where the great kitchen garden was a daunting responsibility. At Ham House, itself a microcosm of architecture and furnishing of the late seventeenth century, the contemporary garden had all but disappeared – a fate which had also overtaken most of the original colour schemes at Hidcote.

Against all this restoration work was set the enjoyment of going round the gardens which came into the Trust's hands in their full glory – such as Blickling Hall, Packwood and Knightshayes Court. Another sort of enjoyment was found in the creation of new gardens where none existed – such as at Moseley Old Hall and at Mottisfont where the disused kitchen garden was redesigned to take the Trust's collection of nineteenth-century and other historic roses. Here, just when we were getting things straight, boundary walls collapsed or needed repairs, and the same happened at Powis Castle. Imagine any one of us possessing, say, a superb herbaceous border, having to empty it so that the wall at the back could be taken down and rebuilt; or the disturbance and traffic caused in dredging lakes at Sheffield Park, where the areas were so vast that a causeway had to be built across the drained lake in order to remove by lorry and truck many feet of accumulated mud.

Seldom a year goes by without some such great disturbance happening in one or more of our gardens. These problems are overcome by team work. It would be useless for a garden adviser to offer advice without capturing the goodwill of the garden staff. And they in their turn have gained the trust of their immediate superiors, the Regional Directors, Historic Buildings Representatives and the Land Agents. This is not all; money is always scarce in an organization which is pledged to spend all its income on tending and improving its properties. Budgets have to be prepared a year in advance if possible. Always the garden staff has to make good, if possible, in time for the season's opening date.

Sometimes, in the smaller gardens, it is the tenant who with or without a gardener has to cope with such work. It should be remembered that whenever possible big jobs of garden renovation or disturbance are timed to be done when the gardens are closed for the winter. (Some gardens, of course, are open throughout the year.) Then, when the days are short and the weather unpropitious, the digging and delving, the major prunings and plantings and the renovation of lawns, path-surfaces and drains have to be done so that all will look well again for the coming of spring and summer – as indeed it does in the accompanying gallery of pictures. By visiting the gardens in different weeks of the year all of us may be present just at the one moment when a unique plant may be at its best. Seldom shall we go away disappointed.

INTRODUCTION

Priest's House, Muchelney, Somerset

The National Trust owns a vast range of different types of garden, each with its own character and historical associations. It is a marvellous collection of gardens for a landscape designer to consult for reference and inspiration.

Garden design is a mirror of custom, history and fashion. The earliest descriptions of gardens are poetic interpretations of the Garden of Eden, totally removed from reality and probably inspired by a beautiful clearing in a wood. These idyllic images were of a garden where fruiting trees flourished and flowers of all kinds filled the air with their fragrance. There might be a temple or an altar raised to the spirit of the place – the *genius loci* or local god – or perhaps water raging over precipitous rocks or a quiet stream wandering through the wild flowers and grasses. Man had no place in such an image, and when he created his own garden he found it necessary to tame the romantic wilderness and protect it from the intruder, to cultivate it in an ordered fashion and to enclose it with hedges or walks.

The earliest gardens were practical enclosures used mainly for food production; then came the medicinal gardens of medieval monasteries. Later still the image of the idyllic garden inspired man to more ornamental improvements. In Tudor times gardens were usually firmly enclosed by walls and within this rigid perimeter were divided into different areas by straight paths or covered walks from which the gardens could be viewed. A knot garden was often placed near the house so that it could be enjoyed from above. There would be an orchard and beds for medicinal and culinary herbs and shrubs. Plants were chosen for their scent or medical purpose and evergreen shrubs were clipped to form topiary figures that could be admired at all times of the year.

As life became more prosperous and secure gardens became larger. In Renaissance Italy classical study led to the rediscovery of the styles of ancient Greece and Rome while a new wealth allowed magnificent gardens to be constructed. The Renaissance garden was an extension of the architecture of the house and indeed was architect-designed. Beautiful statuary and stone fountains, balustrades and steps ornamented the classical designs where formality and order were all important. Such gardens were a great influence and source of inspiration to others. In England we see their impact at Hatfield House where in the original plans water-works, statuary and flights of steps decorated elaborate gardens. Another, more restrained, example was the garden at Ham House, now recreated by the National Trust.

By the seventeenth century there was an increased knowledge of and availability of plants. The Dutch exported many flowering plants and evergreens to England; from France came pleached limes and the elaborate training and pruning of fruit trees to form espaliers. The English passion for collecting exotic foreign plants brought the first botanical gardens in this country.

In the eighteenth century English taste moved away from regularity towards an artificial naturalism – striving once again for the Garden of Eden. The Romantic movement in landscape gardening was influenced by the writings of Alexander Pope and manifested in the designs of William Kent, 'Capability' Brown and Humphry Repton. These eighteenth-century landscapes were great works of art, their creators achieving with water, trees, earth and masonry what artists were representing with oil paint. They were inventing the ideal landscape; creating a paradise on earth.

Henceforth the English love and interest for plants increased; expeditions were undertaken to faraway countries and large quantities of trees, shrubs and plants were introduced into English gardens. With this increasing availability of plants and the greater wealth brought by the Industrial Revolution, the 'natural' landscapes became more elaborate. The grand designs of Victorian gardens, of which Biddulph Grange is an example, had a mixture of all styles and an enormous variety of plants, and were conceived on a large and intimidating scale.

There was a brief return to a more formal mode, but the so-called 'natural' style reached its zenith in the late nineteenth century with the appearance of William Robinson, writer, gardener and author of *The Wild Garden*. Gertrude Jekyll was strongly influenced by his vision of the English cottage garden. A renowned plantswoman, with an artist's training, she skilfully selected plants and colour schemes, the quality of her planting providing a counterbalance to Robinson's more extravagant ideas. She also married architectural formalism with natural planting in her work with the architect Lutyens.

The English Style – well-known and admired all over the world – is the result of a combination of factors: political stability, wealth, a mild climate suitable for plants from many habitats, the English love of the countryside, and, most important of all, the blending of two principal influences – the idea of the natural Garden of Eden and the Hellenic concept of the ordered man-made garden.

The finest gardens of Britain can be said to belong to one of four broad groups: the eighteenth-century landscape gardens, preserved in their original form as much as nature allows; modern recreations of earlier styles as can be seen at many National Trust properties; gardens in which a balance is struck between the formal Italianate style and the Robinsonian wilder garden; and finally the woodland gardens, with their beautiful and exotic collections of shrubs and trees.

Hidcote is a fine example of the third group, a masterpiece of skilful planting combined with an astonishing array of gardening ideas. Although the framework is severe and the Italian influences evident, Lawrence Johnston's masterly planting in the natural English style makes the formality approachable and human. Views into the landscape bring the countryside into the garden so that contact with the natural is never lost.

Sometimes the National Trust has had to create a garden – where none existed – to suit the particular period of a house, for example at Little Moreton Hall and Moseley Old Hall. These accurate reconstructions based on careful research give the visitor a close idea of what a garden would have looked like at a certain period, both in design and planting. Of course many of the gardens featured here are not intended to be historically authentic, being the personal creations of individuals and families. However, whether large or small the gardens are all structured and balanced, some severely geometric and others more romantic. But however formally laid out the love of plants and the natural is always apparent.

My first consideration when designing a garden is the architectural structure of its different areas. These will usually be formal, but softened by shrubs and flowers. I like big flowerbeds near the house, which should emerge from a cloud of flowers – beneath the windows and bordering the paths; clipped evergreens can be used as a contrast to the looser plants. Each garden has a special character, given either by the setting or by the style of the house. It is important to grasp the 'feeling' of a setting and to develop it. In so doing it is sometimes necessary to change existing features in a garden because they are alien to the place; or additional emphasis may be required to give a design more impact. Scale is all important – in architectural structures, in garden features, in the size of the trees and vistas and in the shape and size of the flowerbeds. Formal terraces and steps leading from a house to a lawn or flower garden must be in scale with the house and the space surrounding it. Scale can also be used to surprise or even to frighten. The designer can develop his imaginative ideas by emphasizing or reducing in importance certain features of the design. For example the exit from a long narrow covered walk into a large open space can be visually very exciting. Awe and expectation turn to surprise and a delightful feeling of freedom.

Formal design does not refer only to grand avenues, stone terraces, box patterns or knot gardens, it is the geometric placing of paving, paths, flowerbeds and trees. This principle can be used on any scale, right down to the smallest of town gardens. There is always scope for dividing a space visually, by the use of paving or grass, or by the planting. The smaller the area the more important becomes the pattern and of course the use of plants to emphasize the salient features of the design. The size and shape of spaces and the choice of plants also describe the mood you wish to convey. A natural garden may be part of the overall design but more relaxed in style, where other features like winding paths, rocky outcrops and streams can be introduced. An example is the bog garden at Upton House below the formal terraces. In this garden you can admire the choice of plants, the juxtaposition of leaves and colours, contrasting with each other in the dappled shade of a variety of trees.

Interesting effects can be achieved by the clever combination of plants and colours or sometimes by the repetition of the same plant. Personal preferences inevitably influence the selection. For example, yew and cypress mean gloom and sadness for some but for me they are merely architectural plants that can be placed in strategic positions or clipped to resemble a wall or buttress. A long herbaceous border without the dark green shape of a yew buttress or an upright Irish yew seems to me to lack something, as does a smaller flower border without balls or squares of clipped box. Sensation is important in gardening, for gardens are to be enjoyed. Dull ideas have never produced good design in architecture or anything else, but imagination is a particularly important ingredient in gardening because it is so hard to anticipate at the moment of planting how a garden will grow and ultimately develop. From the photographs in this book you can reflect how very successful many garden designers have been.

PUBLISHER'S NOTE

This book features a selection of National Trust gardens in England; a more comprehensive survey, including properties in Wales and Northern Ireland, can be found in *Gardens of The National Trust* by Graham Stuart Thomas.

ASCOTT

Buckinghamshire

This giant topiary sundial is more a feature of charm than of scientific interest. The Roman numerals of the dial are cut in box and the motto, 'Light and shade by turn but love always', is cut in variegated yew, as is the giant central gnomon.

Ascott was a seventeenth-century farmhouse, which in 1874 Baron Leopold de Rothschild acquired as a hunting lodge. He enlarged the little farmhouse and made extensive plans for the garden with the help of Sir Harry Veitch, head of the famous Chelsea nursery James Veitch and Sons, and the garden architect Walter H. Godfrey. The main features seen today seem to have been completed by 1900. The importance of structure and of special features in garden design is particularly obvious when visiting Ascott where the framework remains intact despite the many years that have passed and the many changes that have taken place. The house and garden were to be enjoyed mainly in the autumn and winter and therefore evergreen shrubs and trees were used extensively. Golden yew and box, variegated hollies, silvery shrubs and magnificent trees make the garden glow at all times of the year and help one forget the bleakness of a grey winter day. Hedges, topiary and formal features lead you through a variety of different enclosures round the southern perimeter of the garden, below the sweeping lawns that descend from the house.

• BENTHALL HALL •

Shropshire

With the exception of the northeast wing, which was a later addition, Benthall Hall remains more or less unchanged since the sixteenth century. The warm sandstone walls, together with the unusual pentagonal bay windows, rising through two floors, and the asymmetrical architecture of the house all add to its charm.

The surrounding garden is of great interest. A collection of crocuses (including *Crocus tommasinianus* and *Crocus vernus*), planted by George Maw about a hundred years ago, have naturalized in the rough grass together with clumps of martagon lilies. The terraces and rockeries are abundant with unusual flowers; *Aralia elata* spreads its leaves over smaller plants and an acanthus marks its position with architectural beauty. Tall plants like veratrums and *Lilium pyrenaicum* add variety to the rocky banks. The pool garden is planted with roses, including 'Felicia', a Hybrid Musk of outstanding quality with pale pink flowers, and 'Grüss an Aachen', a wonderful double-quartered creamy blush rose. Two varieties of the much sought after *Paeonia suffruticosa* thrive against the dovecote walls. Originally cultivated in China and Japan, the double pink peony and the larger, single white one, both of which have a characteristic black blotch at the base of each petal, are a delight to any plant collector.

English lavender clothes and edges these dry walls, its mist of purple flowers and shimmering leaves a natural contrast to the clipped shapes of dark yew. In its natural habitat lavender grows in crevices and on stony ground. The plants like to bake in the summer sun and need a well-drained soil.

Water features, however small, are an eye-catcher in any garden. In the East, water is the symbol of life and no garden can be without it. These charming small rectangular ponds descend two steps of the terraces. A sundial stands above, whose reflection can be glimpsed in the water.

The flowerbeds are punctuated by simple but solid clipped standard box and yew. These are the only features that give the added dimension of height to a garden of low plants. Benthall church, originally built as a private chapel for the Hall, can be seen in the background.

Small geometric beds surrounded by box or other edging plants have been used as features in garden design since Tudor times. In those days dwarf clipped box was planted to create a pattern of flowers. Small hedges have subsequently been employed in other ways, to edge a path or surround a feature or to contain formal beds with larger shrubs and herbaceous plants. Here, clipped box restrains the effusive growth of *Perovskia atriplicifolia*, whose blue spikes shoot up behind newly planted bushes of the China rose 'Mutabilis'.

• BIDDULPH GRANGE •

Staffordshire

In the urban landscape of Staffordshire an overgrown and almost forgotten garden lies buried behind a Victorian building of vast dimensions that at the time of writing is an orthopaedic hospital. Eccentric would be a poor word to describe this lost garden where the association of the natural and the artificial reached its apogee.

The gardens at Biddulph Grange were created in the 1850s by James Bateman on inhospitable swampy moorland on the borders of Cheshire and Staffordshire. At this date a reaction against the 'natural' landscapes of Capability Brown and Repton encouraged many wealthy landowners, whose fortunes were derived from the Industrial Revolution, to develop a profusion of original ideas in landscaping as well as in architecture. Thus the imaginative owner of Biddulph Grange created a garden that contained as many different styles as suited his eclectic taste. He built a huge mansion and within fourteen acres created a profusion of different garden areas. Balustraded terraces and steps in the Italian manner lead to a small romantic lake, while an Egyptian scene cut in gigantic yew topiary depicts a tomb whose entrance is guarded by stone sphinxes. After penetrating this exotic entrance the visitor finds that he has emerged from a Cheshire cottage. Another area, called 'the region of China', can only be reached through a rocky tunnel and a now derelict stumpery, and is complete with miniature lake, bridge, pavilions and a multitude of exotic trees and rocky banks.

The gardens at Biddulph Grange are a testimony to the energy, skill and horticultural interests of its Victorian creator, but they are at present in a bad state of repair. The Trust hopes to raise sufficient funds to undertake their complete restoration.

Massive stones are assembled to form an impressive arch. The search for excitement is apparent in this part of the garden where exaggeration in the scale of structures such as this gate can be in awesome contrast to the miniature perfection of many other features.

A weird frog, which should be poised to leap from a wall, is now restrained on the ground by an elaborate stone edging. Amusing and somewhat frightening features are suddenly encountered when you enter the silent region of 'China'.

The entrance to 'China' is difficult to find from the outside; you reach this mysterious world through a long rocky tunnel or by a winding path through a stumpery – now a lost feature. Looking across a tiny lake you see a pavilion and the elegant arch of a once exquisite red-lacquered bridge, throwing its reflection in the still water.

From the crimson-painted pavilion the visitor looks out on to the stillness of the lake and across it to the small bridge engulfed by rocky banks, shrubs, exotic trees, and clumps of bamboo. 'China' is a self-contained garden in miniature, a jewel and masterpiece of its kind.

BLICKLING HALL

Norfolk

As you wind your way through the countryside the first sight of Blickling is truly romantic. Suddenly revealed before you is the gabled, rosy red hall, rising beyond a closely mown lawn bordered by long yew hedges. The drive ends in a forecourt enclosed by projecting office wings and you enter the Jacobean house by way of a balustraded bridge, guarded by two bulls supporting shields, across the dry moat now transformed into a sheltered garden for tender plants.

The gardens of Blickling Hall are beautiful and vary in style from the Romantic landscaped park and lake, which were probably redesigned by Repton, to the splendour of the avenues of turkey oak, beech and lime, and the formality of the sunken lawn and parterre.

The parterre, which lies to the east of the house, was originally laid out in the nineteenth century and was so elaborate that Lady Lothian, who had commissioned it, had to employ an army of old age pensioners to maintain the vast array of small beds and complex topiary. Later, in about 1930, it was simplified by Mrs Norah Lindsay. Four large square beds with an acorn-shaped yew at each corner were retained and planted with herbaceous plants graded in height. The dense yew hedges shaped as 'grand pianos' were also kept; they sit solidly on the lawn surrounded by carved stone urns. Beyond them a straight path bordered by rhododendrons, azaleas and small trees leads to an eighteenth-century Doric temple at the far end of the woodland garden.

The carefully graded colours of these hardy perennials range from blue and mauve to pink and white. Blue *Echinops ritro* mingles with *Aconitum napellus* and purple lythrums. Erigerons form a mound in the foreground, and the surrounding narrow rose beds are edged with catmint. As the light fades away at the end of a hot summer evening the flowers release their sweet perfume, their colours shimmering in the fading light.

The famous square beds on the main lawn were simplified by Mrs Norah Lindsay and replanted according to a strict colour scheme. The two beds away from the house are predominantly yellow and orange while the nearer beds are planted with pink, blue, white and mauve flowers. The colours and plants are subtly chosen. Symmetrical beds surround each square, planted with red and pink roses to unify the scheme, while clipped yews mark the corners.

These thick and flat 'grand pianos' sculpted in yew catch the sunlight and project their strange shadows across the lawn and gravel. The effect of light and shade is stunning as the shadows follow the sun. So contrived are these green shapes that they become the dominant feature of the parterre and emphasize the ornamental aspect of the formal gardens.

Long and narrow herbaceous borders are difficult to plan, but in this case the retaining wall behind is low enough to allow the upper border to merge visually with the one below. Also the intermittent placing of clumps of bright-coloured plants, such as the gaillardias in the foreground, breaks the monotony of the long border.

Castle Drogo

Devon

Castle Drogo is built on breathtaking terrain. The bare castellated structure rises grimly on the edge of an escarpment above Chagford Vale and the River Teign. It is built in dressed local granite and firmly anchored to the underlying rock. This mock medieval building was created by Edwin Lutyens for Julius Drewe, a man of ample means. It was finished in the 1930s and is the last private house to have been built on such a scale in Britain. It is also a tribute to a successful co-operation and friendship between architect and client.

The structure of the garden was designed by Lutyens and George Dillistone, who was also responsible for the planting. Gertrude Jekyll's planting plan was not accepted on this occasion. The approach to the castle has been kept wild and open in character and the garden is set out of sight of the house. Leaving the house behind you a path leads eastwards uphill to a rose garden surrounded by stone retaining walls, above which are herbaceous borders, hedged with yew. In each corner is a square topiary 'tent' covered with *Parrotia persica*. The path continues on up to a higher level planted with azaleas, magnolias and other shrubs, and emerges on to a large circular lawn surrounded by yew hedges. The garden is remarkable in its architectural severity, which is emphasized by the clipped hedges and stone steps. This striking garden does not have the intimacy of many famous English gardens, but it has clearly stood the test of time. Its disciplined austerity makes it a fascinating garden for anyone interested in design.

The unusual rose garden has a chequered design of square rose beds at the corners of the rectangular lawn, which is surrounded by more beds and a raised border behind a retaining wall of granite. 'Rebecca Claire', 'Amber Queen' and 'Pink Favourite' can be seen in the foreground of the photograph. Tall yew-hedge cubes at the four corners of the garden dominate the scene. The overall effect is one of strong formality and is very modern in concept.

Changes in level are emphasized by the severe design of the steep granite steps whose bare sides are here strengthened by clumps of hostas and the bold leaves of *Filipendula purpurea*. The coral pink of these flowers looks particularly well against stonework in the afternoon light.

Perhaps inspired by his work at New Delhi, Edwin Lutyens designed this Indian motif to run through flower borders. It is a geometric combination of straight lines and curves, which forms a sinuous path. The planting in the adjoining beds is kept low and uniform so as not to lose the impact of the design.

The theatrical layout of this garden is emphasized by the long axial path, which travels upwards through retaining hedges, shrubs and trees towards the rising sun. Massive stone steps break the monotony of the long avenue and the foreground is planted with lavender beds edged with santolina.

Tucked away in a woodland glade is this charming red-roofed Wendy house. A crazy-paving path, which can look so wrong in a grander setting, is here charmingly combined with a simple palisade to provide a cottage garden for the children of the family.

Here is an example of the skilful use of traditional materials in a modern landscape design. The small but solid wooden gate determines the end of the garden and frames the colonnade of beech trees, which in their turn entice the visitor forward into the rural landscape beyond.

CLIVEDEN

Buckinghamshire

Formal gardens and terraces richly furnished with statuary and stone ornaments play only a small part in the beauty of the gardens and landscape at Cliveden. Since the late seventeenth century the various owners have pursued their creative talents in changing and improving the house and grounds. The house as seen today was designed in 1850 by Sir Charles Barry for the Duke of Sutherland, who was also responsible for the enormous parterre below the double staircase. Only a few earlier buildings remain, the Octagon Temple, 1735, and the Blenheim Pavilion, *c.*1727, both designed by Giacomo Leoni. The grounds, like the house, underwent changes throughout the years. Straight walks enclosed by trimmed hedges were at the height of fashion in the 1720s when the famous gardener Charles Bridgeman planted the yew walks; later in the century they were left to grow wild when 'natural' landscapes were in vogue. The evergreen oaks in the ilex grove nearby may be survivors of a plantation Bridgeman created for Lord Orkney.

During the nineteenth century more areas were improved and finally Lord Astor undertook major changes and additions. During his travels in Italy he bought a great collection of statues, sarcophagi and urns, but most beautiful of all was the balustrade removed from the terraces of the Villa Borghese in Rome. He laid out the long garden with its eighteenth-century Venetian statues and created the water garden with the Chinese pagoda, made for the Paris Exhibition of 1867.

The twentieth century has seen the latest addition to the gardens at Cliveden. A rose garden was designed by Geoffrey Jellicoe. Tons of poor soil had to be removed and replaced with loam before the roses could be planted.

As you walk through the gardens and grounds, which have seen so much history and change, you cannot help feeling proud of man's skill and continuous urge to embellish. When the second Duke of Buckingham bought the property in the 1760s, he laid out the first gardens on a barren clifftop above the Thames. Now these cliffs are famous for their beautiful gardens and magnificent woods.

Ornaments have always been used in garden design as focal points or at the intersection of two paths, to terminate a vista or to indicate that you must stop and observe. Such ornaments were usually made of stone, marble or terracotta and were, as they still are, an essential part of design. This great jar, probably Roman, stands ten feet high on its plinth.

Lord Astor's love of the Italian Renaissance gardens is shown by his design for the long garden, which he laid out in 1900. Two eighteenth-century Venetian statues overlook formal beds of box and topiary leading to a central rectangular space where stand Beatrice, Pantaleone, Arlecchino and Colombina, characters from *La Commedia dell'Arte*.

COTEHELE

Cornwall

Ancient stone buildings make wonderful features in a garden setting. This round dovecote with its mossy domed roof sits perfectly against a green backdrop of shrubs and trees and is reflected in the water of a lily pond.

Cotehele overlooks the estuary of the River Tamar, and is surrounded by a delightful garden that has been laid out on many levels above and below the house. First built in the thirteenth century, most of the house dates from the fifteenth, although there were later additions. The garden design is mainly Victorian, but despite its late development the whole atmosphere is that of a medieval garden, with grey granite walls, cobbled paths and walled gardens of tender flowers.

The lawns of the upper garden have a rectangular lily pond as their focal point, fed by a spring. The simplicity of this design is most pleasing to the eye and sharpens one's appreciation of what is to come. Several interesting and beautiful trees are found here, such as the golden ash, *Fraxinus excelsior* 'Jaspidea'; a tulip tree, *Liriodendron tulipifera*; the tree of heaven, *Ailanthus altissima*; and a Judas tree, *Cercis siliquastrum*. There is an enclosed cutting garden and at the northwest corner of the house a meadow that in the early spring is covered with drifts of exquisitely delicate yellow daffodils. White wisteria flowers droop round an archway in the grey stone wall of the terraced rose garden that runs along the length of the protected east front. Climbing roses adorn the house together with magnolia and a passion flower. Two large magnolias, *Magnolia* x *soulangiana* 'Alexandrina' and 'Rustica Rubra', frame the view down to the valley garden, which drops steeply away below the house, leading the eye towards the pond and the medieval dovecote. Rhododendrons, hostas and *Gunnera manicata* thrive round the pond, while ferns of all kinds have taken over its banks. The feeling of luscious growth within a framework of grey granite walls, so typical of Cornwall, makes a delightful experience.

Felbrigg Hall

Norfolk

Felbrigg Hall is situated only about two miles from the east coast and is protected from the North Sea winds by extensive woods, the foundations of which were planted in the seventeenth century. The garden contains many exotic plants and shrubs, most of them suitable for the lime-free soil, and also good trees such as a red oak, *Quercus rubra*, a tulip tree, *Liriodendron tulipifera*, and a *Robinia pseudacacia*. The park has gone through several stages of planting, but still has traces of the seventeenth-century grand avenues and small woods or *bosquets*. At some stage the fishponds were joined to form an ornamental lake and several estate outbuildings were demolished to bring a sward of grass up to the hall in the style of Capability Brown. Tree planting has continued over the centuries, culminating with the last owner, Robert Wyndham Ketton-Cremer, who put in some 200,000 trees.

The walled garden was laid out in the eighteenth century and in the great English tradition provided immaculate vegetables, delicious fruit and a wide variety of annual and perennial flowers for the house. This kitchen garden is divided formally into beds, bordered with box, and slopes slightly towards the south in order to receive maximum sunlight and warmth. The central gravel path leads to a brick archway flanked by a conservatory and vinery and then on through the orchard towards an octagonal dovecote. In the old days dovecotes were depended upon as a source of food, but also made interesting garden features. Their design varied from rectangular to circular; some were built in the angles of garden walls, others were detached and ornamental.

Straight paths edged with box provide a strong linear framework for this border. The blue-grey crinkly leaves of seakale, *Crambe maritima*, contrast with other less architectural herbaceous plants and catch the eye as the visitor proceeds.

A wooden seat is an interesting focal point at the end of a long vista. In this autumn border the graceful wands of *Stipa gigantea* catch the early sun and make a soft background for the dark leaves and imposing spikes of *Acanthus mollis*.

Until the seventeenth century garden seats were usually made of marble or stone and used as ornamental features in vistas, but by the nineteenth century they had become simpler and were more often made of iron or wood. Cast-iron and wirework seats preceded the Lutyens–Jekyll seats of which this is an example. It is called a wheelbarrow seat and was designed to be easily manoeuvrable.

Silver leaves are often used to moderate strong colours. Here the delicate sprays of *Artemisia absinthium* soften the sharp contrast between purple spikes of *Salvia nemorosa* and bright 'Pink Damask' day lilies. A pink mallow, *Malva alcea* 'Fastigiata', adds softness to the colourings. Later in the season, when the *Cimicifuga racemosa* is in flower, everything else will have faded and the border will present a totally different picture of white flowers and leaf patterns.

GREYS COURT

Oxfordshire

The gnarled trunk of wisteria, a favourite in Japanese gardening, twists its branches over the covered walk, its long flower panicles drooping through the framework.

Greys Court is an enchanting house and garden, situated near Henley on rich limy soil. Along the drive clumps of magnificent trees frame a succession of beautiful views over the Thames Valley. The sixteenth-century house is built of brick, flint and stone and stands on the site of a castellated manor, guarded by imposing towers. There are some very good trees in the gardens, including a huge tulip tree, *Liriodendron tulipifera*, and a weeping ash, *Fraxinus excelsior* 'Pendula'. Facing the house are some old Scots pines beneath which clumps of cistus and rosemary grow profusely. On the east lawn strawberry trees, *Arbutus unedo* and *A. andrachne*, with their cinnamon bark fill the air with scent when in flower. The old walls and outbuildings lend themselves well to a variety of small gardens, which have been established through the years under the aegis of several generations of gardeners. There are areas of Japanese cherries, wisteria, roses and a white garden with magnolias and ceanothuses. In the best old tradition the kitchen garden is very much a part of the plan, delightfully planted with seasonal vegetables and fruit, with a profusion of cutting flowers adorning some of the beds. The gardens are almost surrounded by a ha-ha, to the east of which are a wild garden and maze.

Gunby Hall

Lincolnshire

The gardens at Gunby Hall are a feast for the eyes all summer long, with the borders constantly in flower. The walled gardens are designed to keep up the tradition of productive gardening, as well as being highly decorative. Old fruit trees are trained over walls and pergolas, while others are clipped in pyramid forms and outline plots of vegetables and flowers. The formal garden to the west of the house is enclosed by a double yew hedge. It has a sundial at the centre, surrounded by a lawn and geometrical beds planted with lavender, golden privet and catmint. A huge cedar stands on its own, spreading its branches towards the house, while quantities of roses, both new and old-fashioned, fill the air with their unique fragrance. Beyond the lawns and the cedar lies a dark strip of water with a yew-hedged path running beside it, called the Ghost Walk.

Rosa Mundi, a striking old rose whose crimson semi-double flowers are splashed with pink and white, has been known since the sixteenth century and is a great favourite with many gardeners. Its contained compact shape makes it useful for hedges or formal planting. This small shrub rose is a riot of blooms in the early summer.

There is nothing more delightful than to sit in the shelter of a small pavilion on a hot summer's day watching the bees at work among sweetly scented plants. This summerhouse overlooks a paved garden, whose beds brim with small plants such as santolinas, *Stachys olympica*, geraniums, Cheddar pinks and creeping thymes. A pair of standard honeysuckles are an imaginative feature.

The brick walls of the walled garden catch the warm sunlight and the eye is drawn towards the yew hedges at the end of this straight path. Carefully clipped box pyramids terminate a subtle combination of plants designed to maximize the effect of magnificent clumps of red hot pokers, whose yellows and reds make a dramatic sight against a background of green and soft brick red.

Honeysuckle and yellow *Clematis tangutica* grow rampantly together in this border, which runs along the outside of the walled garden towards a square dovecote with an elegant weather vane. A yellow and white colour scheme predominates here, yellow tree lupins nestle behind yellow roses with white irises and yellow day lilies beyond.

HAM HOUSE

Surrey

A 'Sleeping Beauty house' was the diarist Augustus Hare's description of Ham in 1879. He also described 'the entrance through the gateway to a desolate yard with two old trees and a sundial, and a donkey feeding'. How different it looks now that this seventeenth-century house and garden have been restored.

The impeccable proportions and elegance of the forecourt are complemented by the simplicity of the design and planting. A circular cobbled drive leads to the front steps and encloses a roundel of grass, in the centre of which is a Coade stone statue, the whole being overlooked by thirty-eight busts set in oval niches in the surrounding walls. Between each bust cylinders of bay, like sentinels, lead the eye towards the house where more lead busts are placed in niches. A box-edged bed along the front of the first terrace and four standard Portugal laurels add to the elegant formality of the entrance.

More intricate patterns are discovered on the east side of the house where hornbeam arbours run along the four sides of a pleasing geometric parterre of clipped santolina, edged with box. This parterre, the eight grass squares below the south-front terrace and the wilderness have all been restored to the original seventeenth-century design of John Slezer and Jan Wyck.

A wilderness was a popular seventeenth-century conceit, as is well demonstrated by the reconstruction. Grassy walks in the form of a *patte d'oie* are edged with hornbeam hedges in which field maples have been planted at regular intervals. The paths converge in a central area, forming grassy enclosures within the hedges. Each area is conducive to peaceful thinking and dreaming. Whether you are walking about or sitting in one of the little summerhouses you can admire the wild flowers that clothe the grass in the spring and early summer. These magnificent formal gardens, with their vistas and perspectives, are a perfect setting for an outstanding house.

• HIDCOTE MANOR •

Gloucestershire

The garden at Hidcote Manor has been a great inspiration to gardeners and designers since it was first conceived, the variety of ideas and the intricate architectural design of the various garden 'rooms' having a definite Italian and French influence. Major Lawrence Johnston, born in France of American parentage, purchased the property in 1907. It lies in the Cotswolds, the house being built of local stone in the traditional style of the area. There was no garden of any interest at that time save for a cedar tree and a stand of beeches. More than forty years were spent planning and planting this garden. When one looks through the old photographs one realizes what vision and imagination are needed to create such a work of genius. It is easy to claim that Hidcote is a masterpiece of the twentieth century. With the help of colossal hedges, pleached *allées* and topiary, a number of complex gardens, small and large, were grouped around the main axis. The various gardens were designed to house a quantity of tender and rare plants and to demonstrate their variety of shape, colour and character, each enclosure being carefully and very cleverly planned to stimulate the maximum sensation. Every area is different and unexpected, while the glory of the Gloucestershire countryside can be seen through beautiful wrought-iron gates placed at the end of the long and elegant vistas.

This is a very well-known view of the white garden at Hidcote, one of the several garden rooms. Doves of clipped box mark the intersection of paths between four beds in which a variety of white-flowered plants glitter in the evening light. The nodding flowers of the martagon lily mingle with a profusion of *Campanula latiloba alba*, with *Crambe cordifolia* above.

Red roses, red dahlias and dark purple-leaved cannas are but a few among the variety of plants in the red borders. Red flower gardens are unusual, for even though the eye occasionally craves brightness the aggressive impact of too much red can be unsettling. Here the reds are harmonized by different hues of green in the leaves, grass and hedges. The paler greens combined for example with the dark purple leaves of the cannas produce a truly spectacular effect. *Vitis vinifera* 'Purpurea' climbs the red brick walls of one of the pavilions and bronze cordylines in pots accentuate the tone of this area, but also give it a Mediterranean feeling.

At the far end of the red border two little pavilions built in the Dutch style guard the entrance to the stilt garden – so called because of the pleached hornbeams on stems, which flank a small ornamental lawn. At right angles is the long walk, confined by massive hornbeam hedges, its distant view perfectly framed by one of the pavilions. Here is a place to contemplate and to observe the structured framework of the enormous hedges that enclose more gardens on either side of the grass vista. The combination of architectural features such as these, which have been used to emphasize the formality of the design, with the exuberant and informal planting seen elsewhere, is the essence of Hidcote.

There is nothing more life-enhancing than a green beech tree in the early spring when the leaves burst into life and the majestic grey trunks take on a silvery hue as they dry after the dampness of the winter. The slim elegance of this beech *allée* is another feature at Hidcote. This time the rigid formality of the yew hedge indicates the end of the garden and a gateway leads you into the vista beyond.

Matteuccias and other moisture-loving ferns fill the gaps between euphorbias and *Rodgersia podophylla*. Each plant has been chosen to complement or contrast with the others in colour and shape; the bronze leaves of the rodgersia highlight the bright yellow-greens of the euphorbias as well as being a bold contrast to the feathery fronds of ferns.

King Henry's Hunting Lodge

Hampshire

A rough track through a most beautiful and eerie wood leads to an open clearing overlooked on one side by a small lake and on the other by an enchanting brick façade that stands flat against the advancing trees. This Jacobean-style folly hidden in what was once a royal hunting forest is surrounded by a perfectly proportioned architectural garden planted in the romantic English tradition of Sissinghurst and Hidcote. It was built as a folly in 1740 for the Mildmays, who lived at nearby Dogmersfield Park. Later, as tastes in landscape design changed, the park was reshaped, but fortunately the Hunting Lodge remained forgotten in its silent wood. John Fowler, the famous designer, rediscovered it in 1947 and restored it from a state of near ruin.

The brick house, which has three pointed gables, faces south across the common towards the lake. A series of enclosed areas furnished with statues and other garden ornaments surround a central lawn that is flanked by pleached hornbeams. Umbrella-shaped, standard clipped Portugal laurels mark the point where a path crosses the main axis leading towards two delightful pavilions, one on each side of the garden. Old roses and pale-flowered herbaceous plants overflow in the various beds mingling with grey-leaved plants and the rampant pale green *Alchemilla mollis*. Pyramids of box mark the corners of the beds. At the end of the garden John Fowler built a garden room from which you can admire the lake and the wood beyond, on the edge of which are planted several trees with coloured berries and good autumnal tints.

This pink brick folly stands dramatically in front of the ancient hunting forest like a backdrop to an empty stage set, almost as though waiting for an actor to appear on the scene from behind the wings of high clipped hornbeam.

A tantalizing glimpse of one of the pavilions half hidden by the evening shadows behind the pleached hornbeams; this is a garden of many enclosures, each leading into the next, each perfect in its own right, formal and yet excessively romantic.

A fine statue of a shepherdess stands in the shade of a mulberry tree, looking out across the main rectangular lawn. Agapanthus and white lavender, violas and cistuses fill the narrow border at the foot of the sparsely planted façade.

Hybrid Perpetual roses, golden hops and vines clothe this pavilion set at the back of its own charming enclosure. Two small pear trees are planted in the centre of the lawn on either side of the gravel path and pots of clipped box give this 'room' an Italian touch.

The discreet use of statuary is a tribute to the eighteenth-century tradition. This stone shepherd symbolically guards the main entrance to the garden. There is no feature here that has not been carefully planned to the smallest detail.

In this the most perfect of small gardens John Fowler exercised his talents with exquisite taste, a sense of proportion and a profound love and understanding of garden design. This flower-bed is filled with old-fashioned roses – Rosa Mundi forms a small hedge – while large clumps of agapanthus, another Fowler favourite, throw up their blue heads beside *Alchemilla mollis*. The carefully placed statues, hedges and focal points are striking features in this garden. The planting is simple though no less charming for that. The favourite colours are heliotrope, pink and mauve combined with all shades of green and silvery grey. Clematises climb on walls or over old apple trees together with rambling roses, all adding to the lusciousness of the planting within an extremely contrived structure.

KNIGHTSHAYES COURT

Devon

A massive Victorian house, designed by William Burges, Knightshayes sits on formal terraces before a lawn that rolls down to the Devonshire countryside. Terraces, colossal yew hedges and formal enclosures are a prelude to a wooded hillside beyond. This 'garden in the wood' was created by Sir John and Lady Heathcoat-Amory since the last war. Sir John was an avid plant collector; likewise immensely knowledgeable Lady Heathcoat-Amory had the added advantage of being a skilled amateur designer. Trees were felled, views created and areas opened up for more and yet more planting. Here the lime-free soil and mild climate are perfect hosts for rare trees and shrubs. Magnolia species and their hybrids, tender rhododendrons, such as 'Lady Alice Fitzwilliam', grow beside species of corylopsis, azaleas and *Stachyurus praecox*, and many of the best varieties of acer colour the woodland with autumn brilliance. Rambler roses clamber over trees and add a touch of natural abandon and charm. An enormous variety of plants are used as groundcover – epimediums, hostas, dwarf junipers, ferns and hellebores, while erythroniums show their pretty pagoda-like flowers beneath the taller shrubs. Tall eucryphias enhance some of the beds and together with hydrangeas provide interest and beauty in the late summer. Within the wood there is a clearing surrounded by mature beech and larch, below which nestle large clumps of *Rhododendron augustinii* with their different shades of blue. It is a pretty sight; delicate mauves against the silver trunks of the beech, the soft green of spring leaves shimmering above.

Ceanothuses, abutilons, shrub roses, indigoferas, lavenders, cistuses and tree peonies thrive nearer the house. Clematis varieties and the beautiful *Rosa brunonii* 'La Mortola' cover part of the house walls, while in the beds beneath penstemons and agapanthuses give colour in the late summer. This garden is a treat to visit, not only does it provide a wealth of ideas for the passionate plantsman but its layout and setting are of great beauty. Furthermore, one can well see how this was achieved as a result of the great personal commitment and knowledge of the Heathcoat-Amorys.

Understanding light and shade and making skilful use of the juxtaposition of different surfaces and materials plays a great part in the layout of any garden. The dark, concise shape of yew topiary not only presents different shaded surfaces but is a stately contrast to the softness of the lawn.

The subtlety of this garden lies in its simplicity, which is the hardest quality to implement in any design. Not only does it require disciplined thinking but also great patience and confidence before the end result is achieved. In addition to the pool and the statue two features are prominent – the *Pyrus salicifolia* 'Pendula' and the *Acer pseudoplatanus* 'Brilliantissimum', the latter a tree of very slow growth. It has taken several decades for the design effect of this garden to have been realized.

Steps of all sizes play a great part in the design of the formal areas at Knightshayes, some of which are set on terraces overlooking the Devon countryside. Each formal garden is divided by yew hedges and is elegant in manner. Large steps like these are in scale with the landscape and the spaces they link.

Stone troughs are often used in cottage gardens where every available space is taken over for growing treasured plants, miniature shrubs or small bulbs. This beautifully carved trough is planted with a mixture of *Helichrysum petiolatum* and *Diascia rigescens*. Gardening in containers can be very rewarding when space is limited, a form of cultivation that has been enjoyed for centuries. No Renaissance garden was complete without terracotta pots decorating the rigid architectural design of box hedges, stone steps and balustrades.

LITTLE MORETON HALL

Cheshire

Little Moreton Hall is one of the best examples of half-timbered architecture in England, and is an extremely striking sight as one approaches across the flat landscape. The house was built around three sides of a courtyard, and is surrounded by a rectangular moat. Building began *c.* 1480 and ended about a century later, since when little has been added. As there was no record of the original garden, the National Trust laid out a delightful knot garden in 1975, based on a contemporary design taken from *The English Gardener* by Leonard Meager, published in 1688. The grass patterns are surrounded by ten-inch-high box hedging and gravel paths and are enclosed by yew hedges, with an entrance in the centre of each. The hedge on the west side forms part of a yew tunnel that divides the north garden from the orchard. The carefully planned rectangular beds on two sides of the knot garden are planted with herbs and flowers that would commonly have been grown in the sixteenth century. The border along the front of the house has similar old-fashioned plants.

There is no evidence of an earlier garden but the existence of a mound near the knot garden suggests that there may once have been some sort of formal planting here, for knot gardens were meant to be viewed from above.

Simple geometry in garden design is peaceful and easy to understand. The repetition of this pattern and the controlled use of materials is elegant and appropriate to the setting and to the date of the house. Box hedging is used here in combination with the local white and pale brown gravel, while the grass is well maintained and edged to complete the pattern. The beds nearby are filled with traditional herbs and mixed planting of a kind used in the sixteenth century.

Knot gardens are designed to be looked at from above. Geometric patterns, some intricately interwoven, others quite simple, were sometimes placed directly outside the house so that the fragrance of the flowers and the shape of the design could be appreciated from the windows. Alternatively they were planted in a sunken area, to be viewed from a surrounding raised walk or from a mount. The framework of a knot garden is usually outlined with dwarf hedging and is emphasized by different-coloured gravels, grass, or small scented or medicinal plants.

MOMPESSON HOUSE

Wiltshire

Town gardens have a unique charm, tucked away from the noise and interference of the outside world they are a hidden paradise where trees and plants flourish. Set in the Cathedral Close in Salisbury, Mompesson House has a delightful walled garden. At the front of this eighteenth-century house are two magnificent *Magnolia grandiflora*. At the back, the oblong lawn is surrounded by flowerbeds where herbaceous flowering plants are loosely mixed with roses and shrubs. There is a lavender walk on the west side of the garden, leading to a stone cartouche bearing the Mompesson coat of arms, and running along the east side is a pergola over which grow honeysuckle, clematis and wisteria, with a philadelphus behind. This covered walk leads to a secluded patio, sheltered by an old fig tree and enhanced in summer by a colourful display of fuchsias in pots.

A *Magnolia* x *soulangiana* thrives in front of the drawing-room window. The rose border lies beyond where bloom old roses such as 'Little White Pet', 'Buff Beauty' and 'Grüss an Aachen' and, on the wall behind, 'Paul's Lemon Pillar' with its superb creamy-lemon flowers. 'Climbing Paul Lédé' grows on the house wall, a free-flowering climber with delicious tea-scented buff flowers.

For centuries the original purpose of a pergola was to support vines alone. It took a long time for it to be realized how convenient and attractive such a feature could be in garden design. Here stone columns support wooden beams to form an attractive covered path along the length of the garden. Honeysuckle clambers up the pergola and its scent, mingling with that of the philadelphus, is intoxicating on a summer's evening.

The early-summer border is full of surprises and delight. Peony 'Bowl of Beauty' opens its magnificent and colourful flowers and irises fill the air with their delicate smell. Some early foxgloves rise through the rosemary bushes and silver-leaved lavender contrasts with the foliage of later flowering herbaceous plants.

Moseley Old Hall

Staffordshire

Moseley played a part in one of the most romantic and adventurous stories of English history. Charles II, after his resounding defeat at the battle of Worcester in 1651, disguised himself as a woodcutter and was sheltered by Thomas Whitgreave, the owner of Moseley, for two days before embarking on his hazardous journey to safety across the Channel to France. This story was dictated by the King to Samuel Pepys after the Restoration.

The house stands in the Staffordshire countryside, but is now sadly encroached upon by the sprawling town of Wolverhampton and the M54. The Elizabethan outer structure was faced with brick in the nineteenth century and the windows replaced, but much of the interior is untouched and remains as Charles II would have seen it. There was no garden when the Trust was given the property in 1962, so a period garden was recreated using sixteenth- and seventeenth-century designs and flowers that would have been familiar to Thomas Whitgreave. Madonna lilies, soapwort, fritillaries, hellebore, tulips, honeysuckle, sweet briar and musk rose have been planted here. The main feature is a knot garden on the south side of the house. It is a reproduction of a design created in 1640 by the Reverend Walter Stonehouse. Beside it runs an arbour, covered in clematis and purple vines, that leads from the front garden to a hornbeam-covered walk and thence to a path lined with nut trees, which adjoins an orchard of quinces, mulberries and medlars. In the front garden, on the east front, finials and corkscrew spirals of box are set in grass rectangles on either side of the box-hedged walk leading up to the house. The beds and the surrounding borders are filled with climbers and shrubs, underplanted with perennials, all of which were grown in the seventeenth century. Old roses bloom here, among them the Apothecary's Rose or Red Rose of Lancaster, the semi-double striped Rosa Mundi and the White Rose of York.

The design of this elegant arbour was taken from *A Gardener's Labyrinth* by Thomas Hill, published in 1577. The frame is covered by the dark-leaved *Vitis vinifera* 'Purpurea' and two species of clematis – the fragrant virgin's bower, *Clematis flammula*, whose profusion of small white flowers turn into silver-grey seed heads in the autumn, and the vine bower, *Clematis viticella*, with twining shoots and hanging, purple, saucer-like flowers. Under the arbour on both sides of the path a hedge of English lavender leads the eye towards the darkness of a hornbeam tunnel.

Seventeenth-century in style, this simple knot garden is planted in dwarf box. Different coloured gravel and pebbles are used to emphasize the pattern, while round-headed standard box trees give height and an interesting dimension to the design. A boxwood hedge surrounds the whole and formally seals it off from the rest of the garden.

MOTTISFONT ABBEY

Hampshire

Little remains of the medieval monastic buildings at Mottisfont except for the *cellarium*, which dates from the early thirteenth century. Fortunately there are accurate records and plans of Mottisfont's interesting history from its early days as a Priory to the Reformation, when it was transformed into a family dwelling, and up to modern times. Mottisfont is chiefly renowned for its famous rose garden planted by the National Trust and housing the national collection of shrub roses grown prior to 1900 (the 'old-fashioned' roses), but there are many other features in the garden of extreme interest and beauty. A constant spring of clear water gushes out of a chalk bowl into a stream that runs into the River Test. The water table is only a foot or so below the surface, which may be one reason for the exceptionally fine collection of trees that grow here. The largest London plane in England, *Platanus* x *acerifolia*, probably at least two hundred years old, shades a vast area of lawn with its twisted branches, which droop close to the ground. When in leaf the branches hide the mottled bark of its enormous double trunk. In fact two planes were planted close together and became slowly united over the years.

Many other features awaken the imagination and add to one's pleasure and interest when walking through the garden: the rustic summerhouse with its thirteenth-century tiles and corbel; the four eighteenth-century herms; the statues and urns placed in many strategic positions; the pleached-lime avenue with its underplanting of pale-blue *Chionodoxa luciliae*; and, on the site of the old cloister, the small box- and lavender-edged parterre, planted with seasonal flowers.

In the walled garden is the marvellous collection of old roses planted by the Trust. Roses gathered by Graham Stuart Thomas during forty years and from all over the world are planted here in formal beds, surrounded by box hedges or by other herbaceous edging plants. The scent and luxuriance of this garden is overwhelming.

The rose garden has four axial paths with a round pond in the centre. Here colonies of *Alchemilla mollis* spread over the brick-edged beds and nearby alpine pinks nestle against the silvery *Stachys olympica*. All associate well with roses but this border has been planted to give some relief to the multitude of roses in the other beds.

'Constance Spry' has exceptionally large, blowsy, peony-like flowers and a strong scent of myrrh. It is lax in habit and must be tied to supports or used as a climber as it is here at Mottisfont. Though it only flowers once it is the most glorious of all climbing roses.

It used to be fashionable to plant roses in solitary confinement away from other plants, and rose gardens conjured images of unattractive and severely pruned sticks growing out of bare earth. Since Vita Sackville-West's day fashions have changed and roses old and new are often planted together with other herbaceous plants to cover every scrap of soil, and are left as loose as possible to flop over their herbaceous companions. Here 'Cerise Bouquet' is set against a tapestry of blue and white star-like flowers of *Campanula persicifolia*. 'Mme Alfred Carrière' densely covers the brick wall behind. This bed has been cleared since the photograph was taken to give access to a new rose garden.

This is a good example of a beautifully planted rose border. The taller roses are trained against wooden pillars while the smaller ones grow in clumps with herbaceous plants pushing their way up between. Different hues of pale pink are highlighted by the darker red rose in the corner. Pale yellow aquilegias are massed together and add to the freshness of the picture.

NYMANS

West Sussex

Nymans was bought in 1890 by Mr Ludwig Messel, who was an inspired gardener and plant collector. As a result the gardens are not only a treasure trove for the plantsman and garden enthusiast but also an earthly paradise for the visitor who just likes to enjoy the picturesque.

The property lies on deep, fertile, sandy loam and is sheltered on all sides by mature trees. The soil is ideal for lime-hating plants and offers perfect conditions for magnolias, camellias, rhododendrons and eucryphias. Through the years the garden at Nymans has acquired a valuable collection of trees and shrubs, including many that were bred here, such as the magnificent flowering tree *Eucryphia* x *nymansensis*.

The house, which was mock Tudor, was largely destroyed by fire soon after the last war. Sad though this was, the ruined walls now offer a romantic background. Wisteria, roses and honeysuckle climb up the grey walls and the trees and hedges nearby add to the picturesque composition. A series of different enclosures and gardens unfold to the visitor – the pinetum, the heather garden, the rhododendron wood, the old-fashioned rose garden – but it is the wall garden that is the essence of Nymans and the most beautiful of all.

The wall garden, which was once an orchard, contains a multitude of treasures, not least the Himalayan *Magnolia campbellii* and *Magnolia sargentiana*, with their stunning pink flowers and silvery trunks. Beneath their dappled shade thrive the sweetly scented *Styrax japonica* and a selection of stuartias, some with the most marvellously mottled bark. Here are also to be found the evergreen *Eucryphia cordifolia* and the deciduous *Eucryphia glutinosa*, both parents of the renowned *Eucryphia* x *nymansensis*, now so popular in many gardens for its comparative tolerance of limy soils. But the most spectacular of all is the handkerchief tree, *Davidia involucrata*, with its pendulous white bracts.

This is a truly secret garden, for the walls, covered in clematis and roses, are hidden on both sides by trees and shrubs. A visit to this wall garden is like entering another world.

Four great topiary yews mark the centre of the wall garden and four paths converge towards them, bordered by annual and herbaceous beds on either side. Clipped evergreens emphasize the formality of a design, especially when set against bright colours and contrasting foliage.

This stately Italian marble fountain is the central focus of the four paths that divide the wall garden into equal areas. Hidden in this enchanting walled enclosure the fine ornament is reminiscent of a Renaissance garden.

OXBURGH HALL

Norfolk

Oxburgh Hall has been the home of the Bedingfeld family since the fifteenth century. It is a romantic, moated house, whose embattled and crenellated walls and towers are mostly medieval, although greatly augmented in the nineteenth century. Castellated turrets also feature along the Victorian kitchen garden wall, which encloses a grassed area planted as a formal orchard with squares of plums and greengages. Medlars and quinces mark the focal points, and the walls are clad with climbing roses and clematises. But the most important feature at Oxburgh is a parterre copied in the nineteenth century from a French design. This intricate pattern is made out of box, filled with santolina and *Ruta graveolens* 'Jackman's Blue', marigold 'Yellow Boy' and blue *Ageratum houstonianum*. The parterre is laid on gravel and yew-tree balls punctuate and anchor the design. Acres of beautifully kept lawns surround the house and an extensive herbaceous border stretches along the entire length of a yew walk beside the kitchen garden.

Scrolls of dwarf box containing annual French marigolds and ageratums form curved patterns of different colours. This intricate French *parterre de broderie* is based on a design from an eighteenth-century French garden book and is set out to be admired and enjoyed from the windows above, without trees or high objects to interrupt the view. The yew topiary, planted to complete the design, is perhaps in lieu of statues.

The intermittent clumps of dwarf solidago provide a welcome interruption in the long herbaceous border. The dark orange-red *Helenium* 'Coppelia' is in harmony with the wall behind and mixes astonishingly well with yellow day lilies and mauve catmint. The grass walk offsets the pale grey leaves of the long nepeta edging.

PACKWOOD HOUSE

Warwickshire

Giant yews at Packwood frame a distant view of the sixteenth-century house with its pointed gables and chimney stacks reaching into the sky. The dramatic atmosphere created by these severely clipped conical yews is in contrast with the rest of the garden, and is a good example of how garden design should be used to create interest, jolt the imagination and excite the senses. This topiary garden was at one time reputed to symbolize the Sermon on the Mount. The 'Master', a single yew tree, stands alone on the mount, surrounded by the four large 'Evangelists' and the twelve great yews known as the 'Apostles', which flank the cross walk.

Trees and shrubs have been clipped to form ornamental shapes since Roman times, being used to take the place of statues or other stone ornaments, or to emphasize distance. The art of topiary was revived during the Renaissance when plants were clipped to resemble porticoes, urns, animals, cones, spirals, balls and temples. This conceit had spread through England by the seventeenth century.

A sunken garden, raised walks and terraces, gazebos and glowing herbaceous borders are some of the other features at Packwood.

In this packed summer border clumps of herbaceous plants are purposely kept small to maximize the colour spectrum throughout the season. The vivid red of *Centranthus ruber atrococcineus* enriches this composition of heleniums, heliopsis, gaillardias and small solidagos. *Lythrum salicaria* in the background subtly merges into other compositions beyond.

Skilfully combined flowers in the imposing borders have been a tradition at Packwood for many years. The object is to orchestrate colours and groupings to make the borders look as natural as possible and to give a continuous display of colour from spring to autumn. This is done by careful dividing and replanting in order to keep the plants in small groups. The mellow brick walls are exquisite and make a good background to this border where yellow flowers combine so well with pinky mauves. Dark colours, such as reds and blues, can be used to reduce space or as focal points: here dark red nicotiana and scarlet *Lychnis chalcedonica* bring the rest of the border into focus.

However small, a stretch of open water adds a different dimension to a garden, creating reflections of light and shadow. This sunken garden has raised beds packed mainly with hardy perennials, supplemented by annuals, spring bedding plants or half hardy perennials when a particular colour of leaf or flower is needed.

Tightly clipped buttresses of yew planted at regular intervals interrupt the monotony of this long wall and make a perfect framework for roses. The strength of this feature emphasizes the boldness of the red roses in particular, while the repetition of architectural shapes unifies the border. The straightness of the bed is outlined by box edging, whose paler, more subtle green foliage contrasts prettily with the dark yew.

• PAYCOCKE'S •

Essex

Clumps of hollyhocks and wreaths of wisteria create a floral arch around this garden door at Paycocke's, while lavender hedges and silver-leaved plants border the red-brick steps to the garden.

The half-timbered house is mostly sixteenth-century, with some later additions. The garden, designed in the early part of this century, is very interesting and charming. It is a long, narrow garden that has been divided into three very distinct areas; as you progress from the house to the small pond at the far end you walk through formal gardens, across the main lawn, and through a kitchen garden and orchard. Close to the house is an area of twenty-four square beds, somewhat in the style of a knot garden, planted with lavender, santolina, *Geranium renardii* and dwarf alchemilla. More lavender edges the path that leads towards the lawn. An oak pergola or trellis runs across the garden, covered with honeysuckle, *Clematis viticella* 'Alba Luxurians', *C. macropetala* and the climbing rose 'New Dawn'. Before it are two mixed beds containing nepeta, hellebores, Japanese anemones and kniphofias; beyond, a gravel path at right angles to the main axis is bordered by two more beds planted with a mixture of herbaceous plants and shrubs – *Stachys olympica* and small euphorbias grow beside tall clumps of dark purple delphiniums and *Geranium psilostemon*. Three steps lead down to the main lawn, which is flanked on the west by a shrubbery and on the east by a bed containing old roses, such as 'William Lobb', 'Pink Grootendorst' and 'Zépherin Drouhin'.

Hidden behind a hawthorn hedge, the orchard and vegetable garden, divided into four plots, is the last area before you reach the waterside. The progression through the garden provides a whole spectrum of visual sensations ending with the vigorous planting of stately gunnera, *Lysichiton americanum* and drifts of yellow flag irises beside the quiet pond.

PECKOVER HOUSE

Cambridgeshire

This beautiful cast-iron gate, half hidden by two variegated dogwoods, entices you to walk through to the walled garden and explore beyond. Walls are a feature of the gardens at Peckover, which being created on a flat and windy landscape had to be sheltered by an extensive plantation of trees. The fertile alluvial soil made the task easy and the trees grew fast and tall. A Maidenhair tree planted about a hundred years ago was the largest in the country until its top was blown out in a gale. Hardy palms grow here among other interesting specimens, such as a fern-leaved beech, a tulip tree, Californian redwoods, *Sequoia sempervirens*, Wellingtonia, *Sequoiadendron giganteum*, a monkey puzzle and a few Lawson cypresses.

Peckover House is eighteenth-century and stands on the north bank of the River Nene in the centre of Wisbech. The main garden is surrounded by walls; paths divide the flower borders. Here from spring to autumn bulbs, herbaceous shrubs and climbers provide a succession of colour and interest. The main path, leading from the conservatory to a summerhouse, is flanked by borders edged with pinks. Tall metal frames have been erected and are now covered with roses. The beds below are filled with every sort of plant mixture ranging from spring-flowering euphorbias and day lilies to roses, lavenders and hyssop and the later caryopteris, Japanese anemones and agapanthus. Michaelmas daisies are the last to flower, a prelude to the cold winter days.

'Pink Cloud' clambers over tall iron supports on either side of the pathway, its branches falling heavy with flowers. The yew topiary beyond gives a glimpse of an enclosed garden in which an oval pond is central and a painted summerhouse the focal point.

'Buff Beauty' rambles over iron frames above a gravel path edged with *Dianthus* 'White Ladies'. Metal hoops, wooden pillars and trellised pyramids are an effective means of displaying climbing or rambler roses that otherwise would be confined to garden walls. Such supports also give height to the flower border.

Sedum spectabile is small and compact in the early summer. Here it is used to edge a circular gravel path and to contain flower borders leading to the small white-painted summerhouse. Early honeysuckle and philadelphus frame the view through this brick arch and fill the air with delicious scent.

This path is edged on one side by mounds of velvety-leaved *Alchemilla mollis*, whose profusion of lime-green flowers contrasts well with the dark shrubs behind and with the brilliant purple of *Campanula glomerata*. The cut-flower border is well ordered and full of surprises to come. In the distance are canes of sweet peas and roses ready for cutting.

POLESDEN LACEY

Surrey

A symbol of Edwardian elegance and luxury, Polesden Lacey stands amid beautiful grounds and houses a considerable art collection. Mrs Ronald Greville lived at Polesden Lacey from 1906. She was not only a brilliant and famous hostess but also a creative gardener. Much of the gardens as we see them today were of her making with the exception of the long terraced walk, which is eighteenth-century. The spectacular beeches that made the walk so unique had to be felled because of disease and old age. New trees were planted by the National Trust and will be enjoyed in their full splendour by future generations. An Edwardian rose garden has been made in what was probably the old walled kitchen garden, where now modern roses and old-fashioned shrub roses grow beside lavender and clematis. The paths that divide this area are covered by pretty wooden pergolas over which roses are trained; the single carmine-pink 'American Pillar' and the paler 'Dorothy Perkins' are a very pretty sight indeed. Different kinds of lavender, ranging from deep purple to white, and an interesting selection of irises are features in other parts of the garden as are the herbaceous borders along an old wall and the rock garden, built of Westmorland limestone.

Walls provide shelter and privacy in a garden but here at Polesden Lacey the device of a peephole gives an extra dimension by offering a glimpse of the world beyond. Roses and the burgundy-red *Clematis* 'Rouge Cardinal' grow on this wall. Achilleas planted in the foreground prevent the spectator from approaching the opening, leaving you more tantalized to see what lies beyond. An armillary sphere, itself composed of circles, can be seen through the circular opening in the wall.

The head gardener's cottage is nearly overrun with Virginia creeper, while *Clematis montana* 'Rubens' droops over part of the building, smothering it with pink flowers. This climber is always a success and is to be found in many lovely gardens. However widely spread, its charm never fails and the higher it grows the more effective it becomes. Peonies, white columbines, and pale pink *Polygonum bistorta* 'Superbum' bloom in the foreground in this early-summer garden.

Single, deep-yellow flowers with long golden stamens stud the dark stem of 'Helen Knight'. The delightful fern-like foliage adds to the delicate appearance of this vigorous flowering shrub rose – which requires little or no pruning.

SNOWSHILL MANOR

Gloucestershire

Snowshill Manor is a sixteenth-century house, which once belonged to Henry VIII's sixth queen, Catherine Parr. The garden, however, is the work of its most recent owner, Charles Wade, who created terraces, walls, steps, sunken pools, wellheads and niches, all in local stone in the vernacular style of the Cotswolds. Situated on a steep slope, this is a garden in the manner of Hidcote, but executed in miniature. Charles Wade left extensive records from which we can follow his creative thinking. The garden is on the site of the old farmyard and its dovecote and other buildings were determining factors in his design. He believed that structure was of paramount importance and used walls and hedges to outline the different garden areas and to provide a background for the plants. Steep steps link the garden 'rooms' and water is a repeated feature. Although they are small and quite well ornamented, the planting in these gardens is restrained. Shrubs and climbers are used with discipline, but decoratively. Clematises grow through climbing roses over walls and arches and many herbaceous plants are planted in unusual combinations. Discipline was also used in the choice of colours; blue, mauve and purple flowers predominate here, and the seats, doors and garden ornaments are all painted in a greyish blue chosen to complement the golden Gloucestershire stone.

Water increases a space by letting in the sky and gives depth by reflecting surrounding plants and objects. A formal sunken lily pond makes an interesting feature in this enclosed garden and is juxtaposed by an antique well.

Charles Wade designed this beautiful ornament – known as the Nychthemeron. It displays a clock dial, and if connected to a clockwork movement would show the path of the sun through the zodiac as well as the time. A well-loved garden will always have features peculiar to the tastes of its owner.

Two stone buildings and a high wall frame this charming rectangular garden. The paved surround accentuates the geometry of the small lawn, and the shrub planting in the surrounding raised beds, though substantial, is a mere addition to the set. The blush single rose is a subtle ornament to the stone well and an elegant foil to the yellow hummocks of *Corydalis lutea* on the low retaining wall.

A GARDYN WALLED AL WITH STOON
SO FAIR A GARDYN WOT I NOWHERE NOON.

This beautifully painted Arts and Crafts figure of St George above a mellow courtyard makes an unusual strike for a bell. Against the golden Cotswold stone a green vine entwines with pale-flowered honeysuckle to engulf a window with their foliage.

TINTINHULL HOUSE

Somerset

Originally built as a farmhouse in the seventeenth century, Tintinhull's elegant west front of Ham stone was added in the eighteenth, and looks out over a series of formal gardens, each with a different character. The framework is structured, but is combined with informal planting. The garden was mainly designed by Phyllis Reiss and even though we know that she was greatly influenced by the Jekyll–Lutyens 'new style', and by Lawrence Johnston, the garden is totally original in the choice and combination of plants. Mrs Reiss used her horticultural knowledge carefully in selecting plants to suit each garden and season so that the visitor is amazed by the quantity of plants in flower at any time. Much of the garden can be viewed from the house and for this reason she felt it important that the borders should display a varying selection of plants throughout the year. The richness and naturalness of the planting makes a visit to Tintinhull a real experience, and a delightful progression as one moves from one 'room' to another. Peaceful areas like the yew-hedged fountain garden, where all is white and silver and the only movement is the gentle ripple on the water's surface caused by a gust of wind, alternate with the gay ones, where bolder plant associations and stronger colours make one realize how successful a daring choice of plants can be.

Pavilions, water features, beautifully laid stone paths, immaculately clipped yew hedges, pleasing proportions and interesting planting make Tintinhull a jewel and a pleasure to visit.

A mist of bronze fennel catches the light in the kitchen garden. Pale green clumps of *Nepeta* 'Six Hills Giant', covered with arching flower sprays of the most delicate lavender colour, edge the gravel path, which leads through a wooden gate to the fields beyond.

Against mellow brick walls in the early-morning light these pale pink roses look as if they are floating above a border of green leaves. The harmonious blending of different greens and leaf shapes gives the border a cool and restful appearance.

Compact roses make charming informal hedges for the less structured layout. Some of the favourites for this purpose are Rosa Mundi, the Rugosas 'Blanc Double de Coubert' and 'Sarah van Fleet', and the Hybrid Musks 'Felicia' or 'Penelope'. This charming hedge bordering a stone path is the Polyantha China rose 'Nathalie Nypels'. It flowers all summer until well into the autumn and is a real joy even in hotter countries where the most prolific of roses finish flowering by August.

No border should ever be completely monochrome, for the occasional contrasting leaf or flower helps to brighten and enrich the main colour.

UPTON HOUSE

Warwickshire

Extensive terraces, lawns, ha-has, hidden gardens and glimpses of an eighteenth-century landscape unfold before your eyes as you wander through the garden at Upton. From the terrace on the garden front, where the double yellow Scots rose, subtly combined with lavender and catmint, contrasts well with the brown Hornton stone of the house, the wide lawns stretch southwards with magnificent trees on either side. It is only when walking away from the house towards a distant meadow that you come unexpectedly upon the main garden, which is hidden in a long valley below.

Skilfully designed steps and landings descend steeply to a rectangular lake. Here are brick ha-ha walls covered in roses and wisteria, herbaceous borders, a kitchen garden laid out in the manner of a French *potager*, old yew hedges enclosing rose beds, all descending sharply towards the lake and nuttery, where daffodils, wild primroses and cowslips bloom in spring. Small plants cling to every crevice of the stonework and the shrubs and climbers, herbaceous plants, fruit trees and vegetables all flourish on the sunny south-facing slope.

To the right of the incline a grand staircase descends graciously, its stone walls and balustrades framed by dark cedars on one side and by the sloping beds on the other, and its steps clothed with purple aubrieta. West of the main garden, and at right angles to it, two square ponds have been drained to create a bog garden and cherry orchard.

To create a perennial border is a *tour de force* of aesthetic feeling and expertise. It is a very personal pursuit on which one can stamp one's own style. Any colour combination can be picked from the vast range of plants available. Mixed borders are at their best between June and September, but it is advisable to concentrate the flowering period to avoid a spotty appearance. Here at Upton a beautifully edged lawn path separates the twin borders. The ground slants towards the water's edge extending the visual impact of this colourful array. Clumps of white nicotiana fill the gaps and lengthen the flowering season. Pink phlox and white chrysanthemums are among the taller plants with neat clumps of sedums and hostas in front.

The flower spikes of lavender vary from light to dark purple, pink and white. The true English lavender is actually a native of the Mediterranean countries, where lavender is cultivated to extract scent. Of the dwarf varieties used for edging paths or beds 'Hidcote' is the darkest, with purple flower spikes, and 'Munstead' is paler with a wonderful scent. Lavender should be clipped in the spring to keep it compact. This long lavender hedge borders one side of a grass walk, while a tall wall rises on the other. *Cotoneaster horizontalis* is trained up it and a variety of shrubs and perennials grow at its foot.

How enchanting it is to meander along a woodland path in the shade of trees and shrubs where plants are allowed to grow unrestrained and to spread themselves at random. But however haphazard and natural a planted woodland border looks, one soon discovers that plants and combinations have been chosen with infinite care. Here broad-leaved hostas in the foreground mark the first bend in the path and emphasize the delicacy of the late-flowering primulas. Clumps of astilbes of different shades stand out against the dark green groundcover plants.

Salix alba 'Britzensis' is colourful in the winter with its brilliant show of scarlet branches as is the golden-twigged *Salix alba vitellina*. Both require drastic pruning in the spring to encourage growth and to produce a profusion of branches for the winter display. These stumps have just been pruned. They are growing in the bog garden, surrounded by drifts of moisture-loving plants and daffodils.

WESTBURY COURT

Gloucestershire

In the open flat fields of the Severn Valley a Dutch garden has been recreated after years of oblivion and decay. With the help of generous donations and grants the National Trust undertook the restoration of this extraordinary formal water garden dating from the end of the seventeenth century. Unlike many other formal gardens it had not been swept away by the wave of natural landscaping in the eighteenth century. An engraving by Kip in *c.* 1707 shows a house surrounded by canals and a formal parterre, but when the Trust took over the property in the 1960s nothing remained of the seventeenth-century garden except the ruins of a once elegant pavilion, a gazebo and the long reed-clogged canals. The canals had to be dredged and their walls repaired. New yew hedges were planted and a copy of the parterre shown by Kip was laid out on the newly sown lawn. The parterre is simple, its pattern of squares, triangles and circles outlined by dwarf box, *Buxus sempervirens* 'Suffruticosa', and ornamented by standard box-tree balls and pyramids. Some of the beds are filled with *Festuca ovina glauca*, others with hardy annuals such as pot marigold, mignonette and love-in-a-mist.

All the planting in the garden follows the original records: there are apples, pears and plums against the long wall to the west of the canals, with fritillaries, narcissi, anemones and tulips beneath them; clipped thorns and Portugal laurels on the lawns, also medlars, quinces and morello cherry trees; and in the borders and small walled rose garden hundreds of herbaceous plants, shrubs, climbers and herbs that would have been grown in 1700 – *Iris pallida*, *Salvia pratensis*, primroses, violets, campanulas and foxgloves, *Clematis flammula*, *Lonicera periclymenum*, moss roses, cabbage roses and sweetbriar to name but a few.

Timing must be one of the most important aspects of garden photography, not only in terms of season, which is obviously the first consideration, but in the timing for each individual garden. One can visit a garden in spring and then return in late summer to find it a completely different place; although the design of course remains the same, the colours, blooms and foliage will all have changed. So the first thing to consider is whether a garden is at its best in spring, early or late summer, as few can be perfect at all seasons.

After the first flush of spring flowers in April and May, midsummer brings the roses, which are the central feature of most English gardens; photography of formal gardens before the roses are in bloom can be a little unrewarding. A visit to Mottisfont Abbey in Hampshire, which has the national collection of old-fashioned roses, during that crucial week in late June when these old shrub roses are in bloom can bring some spectacular results, although the sheer mass of flowers makes it difficult to decide where to set up the camera. Some of the same old-fashioned roses are to be found again several weeks later at Gunby Hall in Lincolnshire, as East Anglia is almost a month behind the south.

Another aspect of the importance of timing is that of time in relation to light. To attempt to convey the subtlety of colour and tone in a carefully planted garden under the harsh light of a midday sun is a pointless task, as the colours will bleach and the form will be lost in the sunlight reflecting from the endless surfaces. The choice of time in relation to light is crucial; my visits to these gardens were whenever possible at the golden hour, those times just after dawn and before sunset when the light is most conducive to photography.

One of the aims of the photography was to convey the quiet dignity of the gardens, to allow the eye to follow box-edged paths through formal beds to some distant statue or astrolabe. In so many ways formal gardens lend themselves to photography, the only danger being that of repetition. To avoid this I have occasionally introduced another element into the photograph – a low sun filtering through leaves as a backlight, or a screen of leaves or an arch or doorway to give a sense of entering into another space. Some of the gardens, like Hidcote, Peckover and Snowshill Manor, which have a series of garden rooms opening into each other, separated by yew hedges, old walls or terraces, suit this approach quite well, each 'room' having a different atmosphere. I found, however, that some gardens had a certain wildness within their formal design, a lushness and unexpectedness inside a rigid pattern that gave a tremendous sense of freedom to the photography. The garden at King Henry's Hunting Lodge had this quality and must be one of the most hauntingly beautiful small gardens in England.

The photographs were all taken on a 35 mm Canon F1 camera, using either a 28 mm lens for the wide-angle shots or a 90 mm macro lens for the close-ups. For the most part I used Fuji 50 ASA transparency film with an 81A filter. This seemed to give a satisfactory rendering of green tones, which was important, while avoiding the poor reproduction one can get from the faster E6 films. Most of the photographs were taken using a tripod to give me maximum depth of focus and long exposures when necessary, without camera movement. Occasionally I used a graduated filter if the sky was too bright, distracting the eye from the main content of the photograph. When I have done this, I have tried to use one that was harmonious with the sky colour at the time.

I have attempted to include most of the smaller formal gardens of the National Trust and to convey an intimacy that is not possible with the larger parklands and vast rhododendron gardens. Two exceptions are Sissinghurst, which is unfortunately so overvisited at present that the National Trust prefer it to be excluded from any publication, and Scotney Castle, where the lake has recently been drained making the garden unfit for photography during the summer of 1986. There will no doubt be other favourites omitted through lack of space, but I hope that the photography will give something of the special flavour that these gardens have, and reflect the care and attention that has been afforded them throughout the years.

Clay Perry

The majority of these gardens are open on a regular basis from April to October, details of opening times may be found in *The National Trust Handbook for Members and Visitors*. However, some gardens are open only infrequently, information on these can be found in The National Garden Scheme guide, *Gardens of England and Wales Open to the Public*, or by application to the National Trust.

ASCOTT
Wing, near Leighton Buzzard,
Bedfordshire LU7 0PS

BENTHALL HALL
Broseley, Shropshire TR12 5RX

BIDDULPH GRANGE
Grange Road, Biddulph, Stoke-on-Trent,
Staffordshire ST8 7SD

BLICKLING HALL
Blickling, Norwich, Norfolk NR11 6NF

CASTLE DROGO
Drewsteignton, Devon EX6 6PB

CLIVEDEN
Taplow, Maidenhead, Berkshire SL6 0JB

COTEHELE
St Dominick, near Saltash, Cornwall PL12 6TA

FELBRIGG HALL
Felbrigg, Norwich, Norfolk NR11 8PR

GREYS COURT
Rotherfield Greys, Henley-on-Thames,
Oxfordshire RG9 4PG

GUNBY HALL
Gunby, near Spilsby, Lincolnshire PE23 5SS

HAM HOUSE
Ham, Richmond, Surrey TW10 7RS

HIDCOTE MANOR
Hidcote Bartrim, Chipping Campden,
Gloucestershire GL55 6LR

KING HENRY'S HUNTING LODGE
House not open to the public.

KNIGHTSHAYES COURT
Bolham, Tiverton, Devon EX16 7TQ

LITTLE MORETON HALL
Congleton, Cheshire CW12 4SD

MOMPESSON HOUSE
The Close, Salisbury, Wiltshire SP1 2EL

MOSELEY OLD HALL
Fordhouses, near Wolverhampton,
Staffordshire WV10 7HY

MOTTISFONT ABBEY
Mottisfont, near Romsey,
Hampshire SO5 0LP

NYMANS
Handcross, near Haywards Heath,
West Sussex RH17 6EB

OXBURGH HALL
Oxborough, King's Lynn, Norfolk PE33 9PS

PACKWOOD HOUSE
Lapworth, Solihull, West Midlands B94 6AT

PAYCOCKE'S
West Street, Coggeshall, Colchester,
Essex CO6 1NS

PECKOVER HOUSE
North Brink, Wisbech,
Cambridgeshire PE13 1JR

POLESDEN LACEY
near Dorking, Surrey RH5 6BD

SNOWSHILL MANOR
near Broadway, Gloucestershire WR12 7JU

TINTINHULL HOUSE
Tintinhull, near Yeovil, Somerset BA22 8PZ

UPTON HOUSE
near Banbury, Oxfordshire OX15 6HT

WESTBURY COURT
Westbury-on-Severn
Gloucestershire GL14 1PD

Clifford, Derek *A History of Garden Design*, Faber & Faber, London, 1966

Dixon Hunt, John *Garden and Grove*, Dent, London, 1986

Hadfield, Miles *Gardening in Britain*, Hutchinson, London, 1960

Hellyer, Arthur *Gardens of Genius*, Hamlyn, London, 1980

Hobhouse, Penelope *The National Trust Book of Gardening*, Pavilion/Michael Joseph, London, 1986

Hyams, E. and Smith, E. *The English Garden*, Thames & Hudson, London, 1964

Jekyll, Gertrude, *Garden Ornament*, Country Life, London, 1918; Antique Collectors' Club, Woodbridge, 1982

Thacker, Christopher *The History of Gardens*, Croom Helm, London, 1979

Thomas, Graham Stuart *Gardens of the National Trust*, Weidenfeld & Nicolson, London 1979

Guidebooks of the National Trust